Nurses
Community Workers

by Cynthia Klingel and Robert B. Noyed

Content Adviser: Dr. Katharyn May, Dean,
School of Nursing, University of Wisconsin

Reading Adviser: Dr. Linda D. Labbo,
College of Education, Department of Reading Education,
The University of Georgia

COMPASS POINT BOOKS

Minneapolis, Minnesota

Compass Point Books
3722 West 50th Street, #115
Minneapolis, MN 55410

Visit Compass Point Books on the Internet at *www.compasspointbooks.com* or e-mail your request to *custserv@compasspointbooks.com*

Photographs ©: DigitalVision, cover; Corbis, 4, 23; Peter Krinninger/ImageState, 5; Photo Network/Tom McCarthy, 6, 14, 26; Unicorn Stock Photos/Jeff Greenberg, 7; James L. Shaffer, 8, 11, 12, 18, 20; Photo Network/Mike Moreland, 9, 13, 21, 27; Unicorn Stock Photos/Mark E. Gibson, 10; Michael Paras/ImageState, 15; Novastock/ImageState, 16; Mark S. Skalny/Visuals Unlimited, 17; Unicorn Stock Photos/B.W. Hoffmann, 19; Warren Morgan/Corbis, 22; Richard T. Nowitz/Corbis, 24; Unicorn Stock Photos/Jean Higgins, 25.

Editors: E. Russell Primm, Emily J. Dolbear, and Pam Rosenberg
Photo Researcher: Svetlana Zhurkina
Photo Selector: Linda S. Koutris
Designer: Bradfordesign, Inc.

Library of Congress Cataloging-in-Publication Data

Klingel, Cynthia Fitterer.
    Nurses / by Cindy Klingel and Robert B. Noyed.
        p. cm. — (Community workers)
    Includes bibliographical references and index.
    Summary: A simple description of the activities, tools, uniforms, training, skills, problems, and importance of nurses.
        ISBN 0-7565-0306-X
        1. Nursing—Juvenile literature. [1. Nurses. 2. Nursing. 3. Occupations.] I. Noyed, Robert B. II. Title. III. Series.
    RT61.5 .K57 2002
    610.73—dc21   2002002954

Table of Contents

What Do Nurses Do?

Nurses do many tasks. They help sick people of all ages to get well. They also help people stay well. Some nurses work with doctors during **surgery** in hospitals. Some nurses help women who are having babies. Nurses called nurse practitioners give patients **checkups.** They also write **prescriptions** for medicine.

A nurse reads to a young patient.

A nurse helps a patient take a sponge bath.

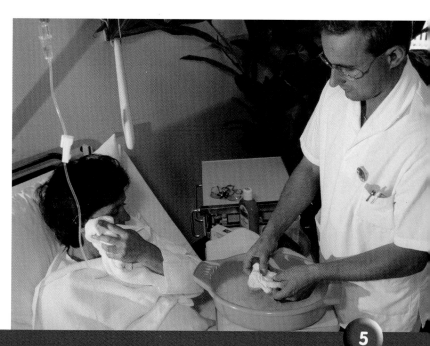

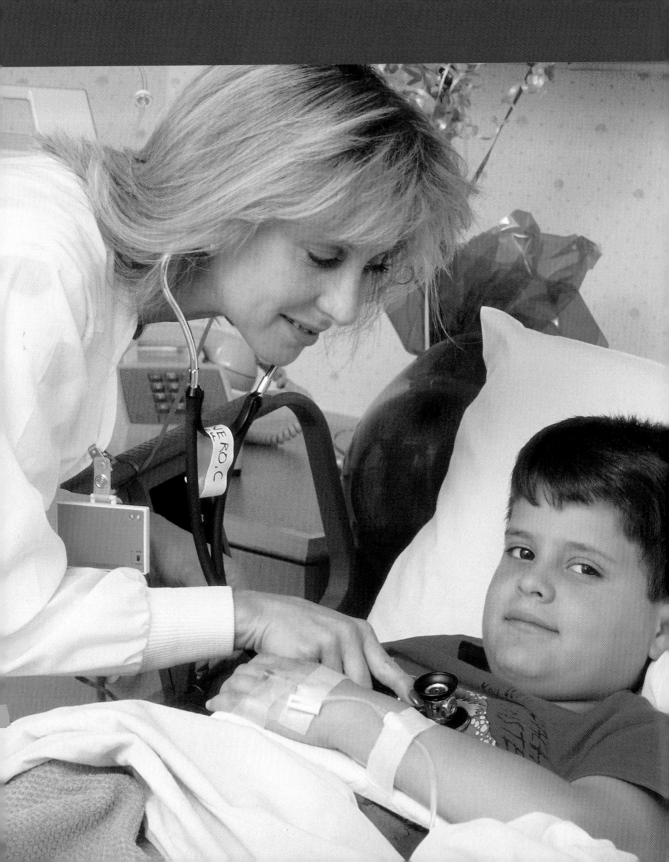

What Tools and Equipment Do They Use?

Nurses need many tools to do their jobs. They use **thermometers** to see if a patient has a fever. They use a **stethoscope** to listen to a person's heart and lungs. A cuff is used to measure **blood pressure**. Nurses write all this information on the patient's chart.

◀ This nurse is using a stethoscope.

A nurse records ▶ information on a patient's chart.

Nurses in hospitals use a lot of special equipment. In the **intensive care unit**, nurses use **monitors** to check on patients' conditions. They use machines to give people the right amount of medicine, too. Surgical nurses use many different tools to help doctors during surgery.

◄ Nurses use machines to help give patients their medications.

A nurse watches computer screens to keep track of patients. ►

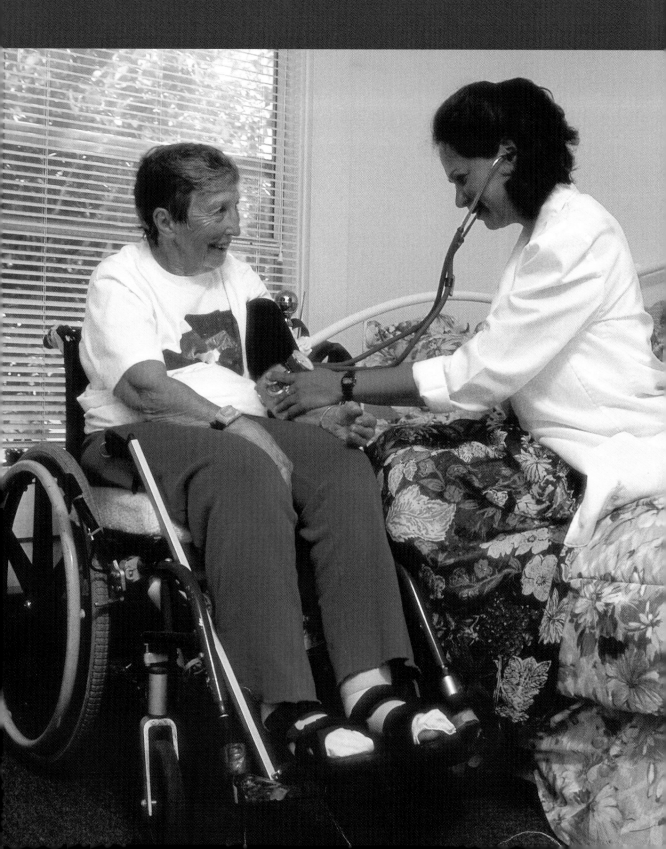

How Do Nurses Help?

People depend on nurses to help them when they are sick or hurt. Do you know someone with a new baby? Nurses teach new mothers how to take care of their babies. Does your school have a nurse? School nurses teach children about eating well and about the importance of exercise.

A nurse checks on a patient who can't leave home.

At health fairs, nurses teach people about staying healthy.

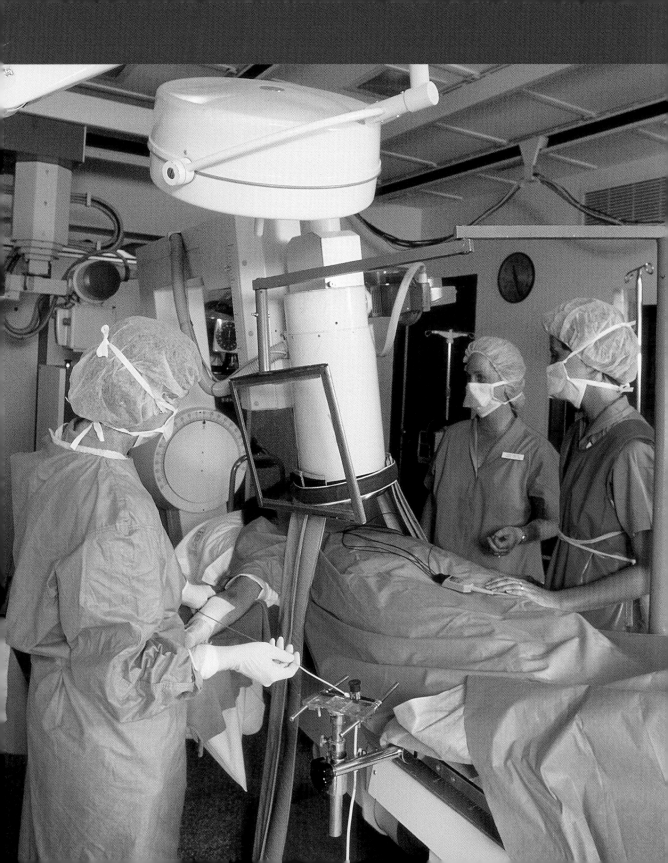

Where Do Nurses Work?

Nurses work in hospitals and in doctors' offices. They work in schools and clinics, too. Some businesses have nurses in their offices or factories. Some nurses visit people in their homes. Other nurses work in the army, navy, or air force. Some nurses teach others how to become nurses.

Nurses assist a doctor with an X ray.

A nurse visits a patient in her home.

With Whom Do Nurses Work?

Nurses often work with doctors. Nurses also work closely with other nurses. They work with nurses aides, too. Nurses aides help nurses take care of patients. It takes teamwork to give patients the best care.

◀ Nurses aides help nurses and patients in many ways.

A doctor (left) ▶ and nurse discuss the patients they are caring for.

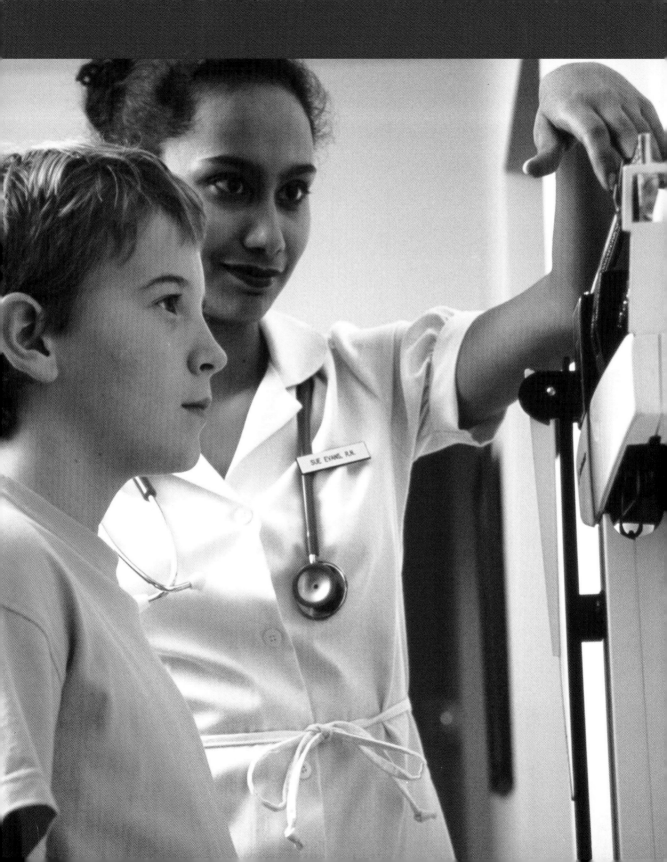

What Do Nurses Wear?

Nurses usually wear a uniform. The uniform is often a shirt, pants, and comfortable white shoes. Uniforms can be white or colorful. Nurses who work in surgery wear a special uniform. They also wear a cap and a mask to protect the patient from germs.

◀ A nurse weighs a patient.

Nurses often wear uniforms called "scrubs." ▶

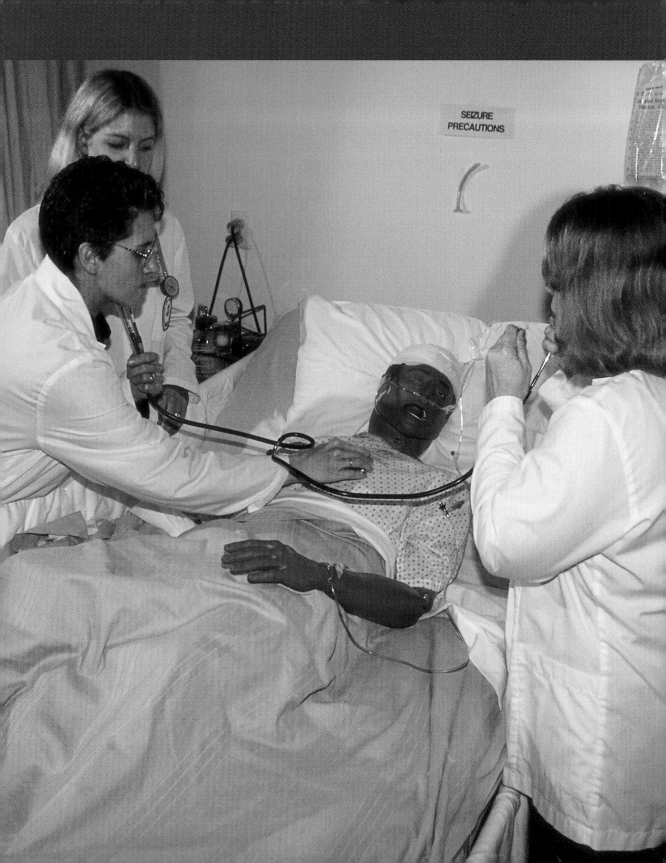

What Training Does It Take?

All nurses need a high school diploma. Licensed practical nurses (LPNs) take nursing classes after high school. Most registered nurses (RNs) have a two- or four-year college degree. Nurses must train in hospitals or community health centers. They must pass a test to become nurses.

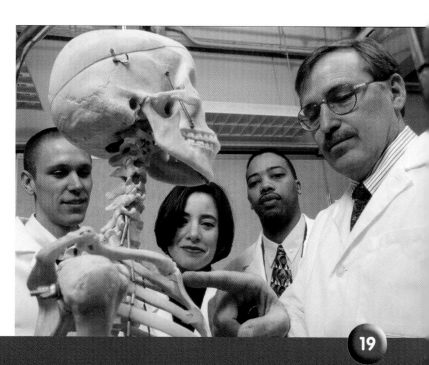

◄ Student nurses train using a dummy patient.

Students learn ► about the human skeleton.

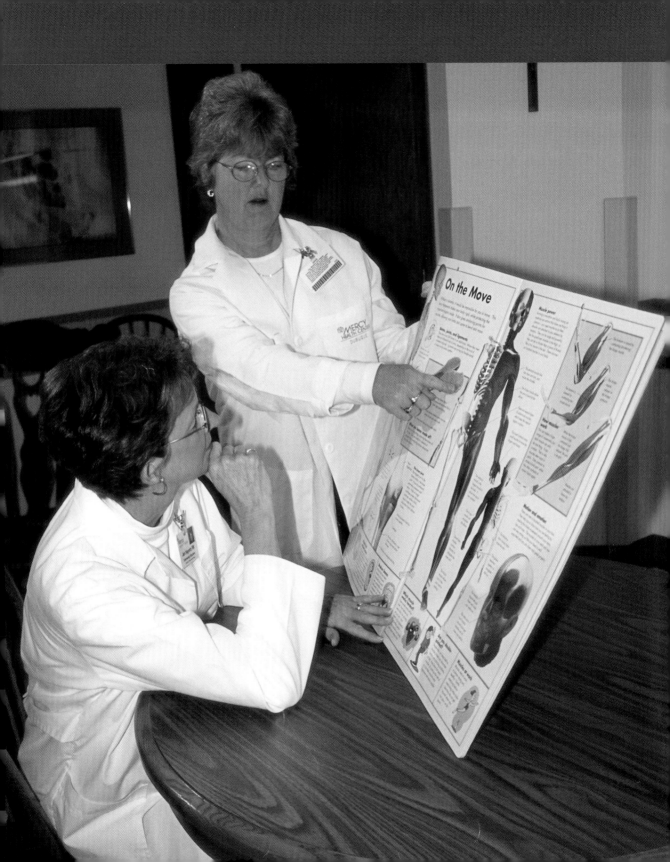

What Skills Do Nurses Need?

Nurses have to be good with details and have excellent memories. They must give each patient the medicine the doctor has ordered. Nurses need to make people comfortable when they are hurt or afraid. Nurses have to be able to do many things at once!

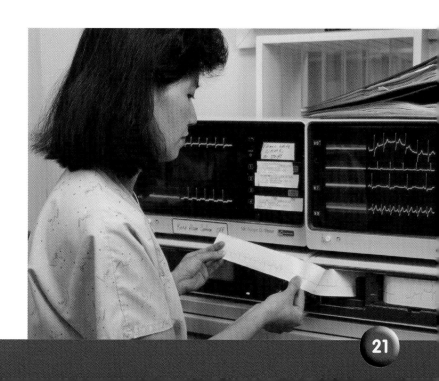

Nurses look at a chart of the human body.

Nurses must be able to use many different kinds of medical equipment.

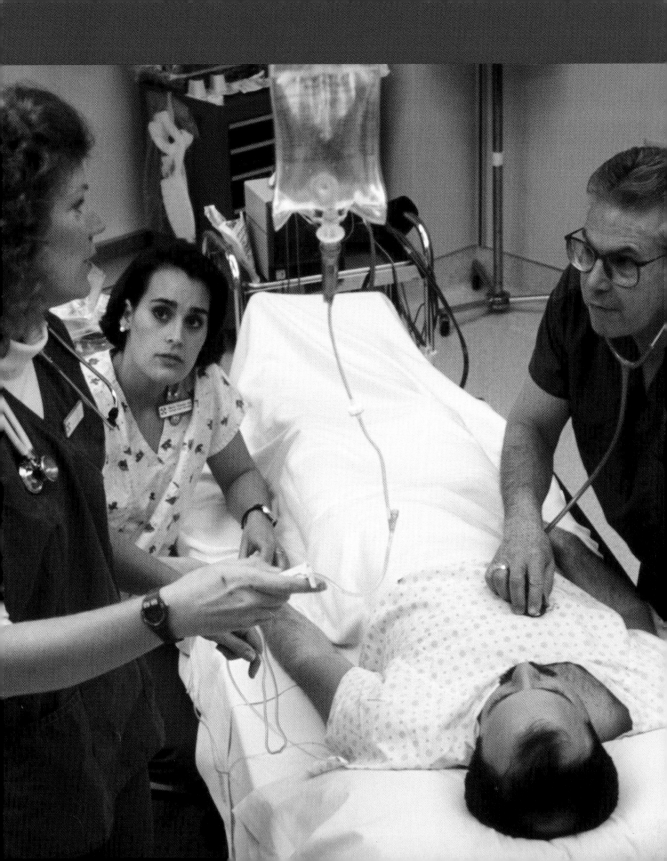

What Problems Do Nurses Face?

Nurses often work long hours. It can be stressful to know that making a mistake might harm someone. Often nurses work with patients who are sick. Some patients die. Nurses have to keep working even when sad things happen.

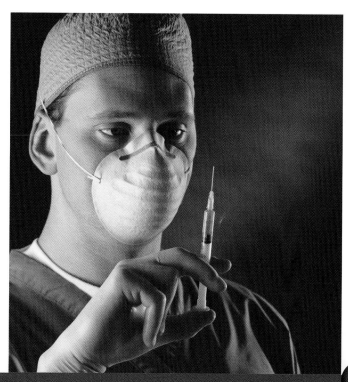

◄ Nurses have to work well under stress.

Medications ► are measured carefully before being given to patients.

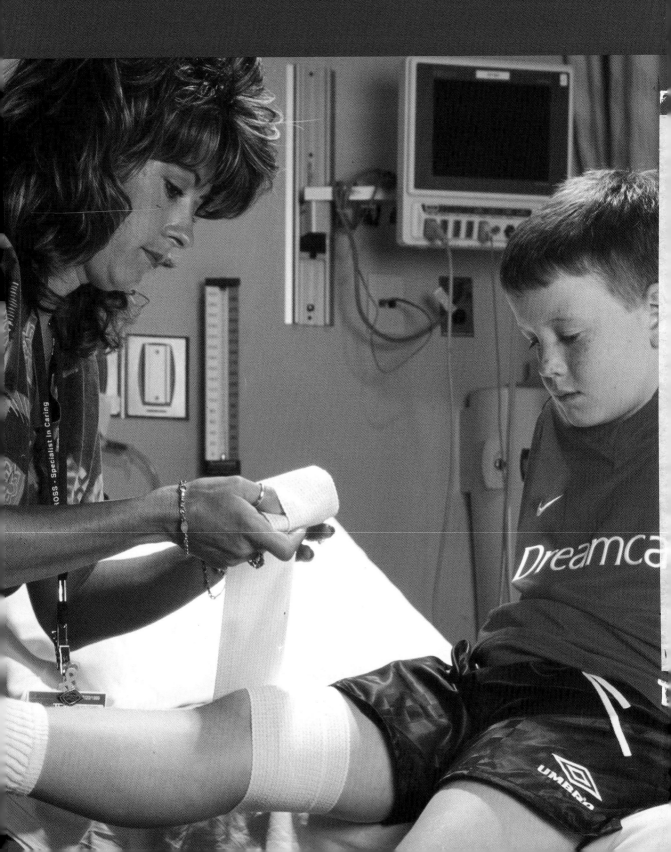

Would You Like to Be a Nurse?

Are you interested in how the body works? Do you like doing things for others? Maybe you would like to be a nurse! You can start now. Do your best in school. Study hard in your science and math classes. Help take care of sick family members. It can be a wonderful feeling to help someone get better.

A nurse bandages a boy's leg.

A nurse offers a treat to a young patient.

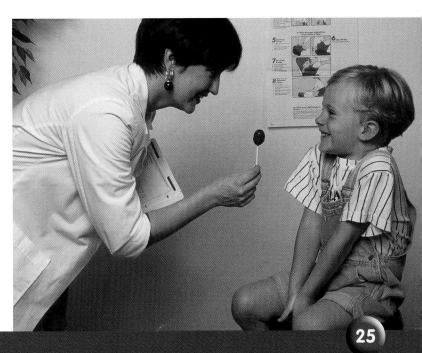

A Nurse's Tools and Clothes

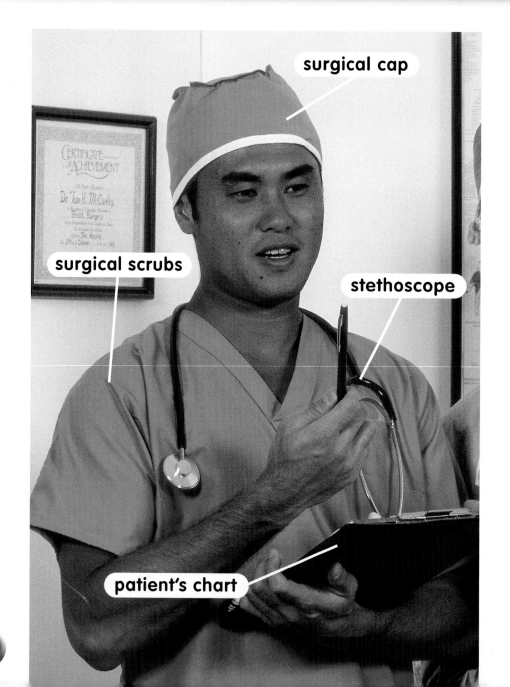

surgical cap

surgical scrubs

stethoscope

patient's chart

At the Hospital

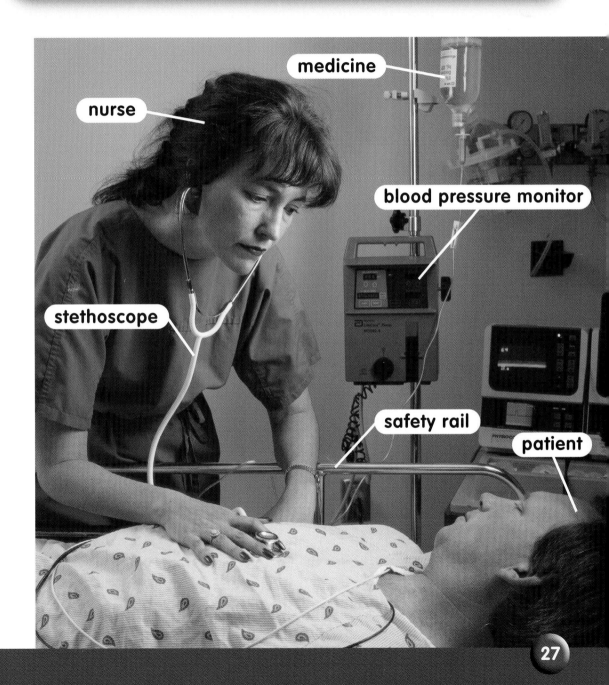

medicine

nurse

blood pressure monitor

stethoscope

safety rail

patient

A Nurse's Day

Early Morning
- Today, this nurse will work the evening shift. In the morning, she reads some nursing journals. They help her learn how to do her job better.

Afternoon
- She arrives at the hospital about 3:00 P.M. and goes to the nursery.
- She checks in with the nurses who worked the day shift. She needs to find out how her patients are doing.
- She checks on each baby and each mother. She makes sure to record everything she does on the patients' charts.
- One mother and father have some questions for the nurse. She stops by their room to answer their questions about taking care of the new baby.

Evening
- She teams up with another nurse to give some of the babies their first shots.
- The nurse makes one last check to see if her patients are doing well and if anyone needs anything.
- Most of the mothers are going to sleep now. The nurse brings some of the babies to the nursery.

Night
- At the end of the evening shift, the nurses who work the overnight shift arrive. They discuss how the patients are doing.
- It is 11:00 P.M. and time to go home. It has been a long day!

Glossary

blood pressure—the pressure of the blood against the walls of the blood vessels

checkups—medical examinations to make sure that patients are healthy

intensive care unit—a part of the hospital where very ill patients are cared for

monitors—machines that keep track of patients' conditions

prescriptions—doctors' or nurse practitioners' orders for medicine

stethoscope—an instrument that allows doctors and nurses to listen to a patient's heart and lungs

surgery—cutting open a patient's body to fix or remove a body part

thermometers—instruments used to measure temperature

Did You Know?

- A British nurse named Florence Nightingale wrote the first textbook for nurses in the 1800s. It is called *Notes on Nursing*.

- The American Nurses Association was created in 1896. This organization represents 2.6 million registered nurses in the United States.

- Between 1096 and 1270, during the Crusades, some knights provided nursing care to the sick and injured.

- More than 1,600 nurses from the U.S. Army Nurse Corps earned medals for their service and bravery during World War II (1939–1945).

- The nursing profession is trying to recruit more men. About 6 percent of the 2.7 million nurses in the United States are men.

Want to Know More?

At the Library

Burby, Liza N. *A Day in the Life of a Nurse*. New York: PowerKids Press, 1999.

Flanagan, Alice K. *Ask Nurse Pfaff, She'll Help You*. Danbury, Conn.: Children's Press, 1997.

Schaffer, Lola M., and Gail Saunders-Smith. *We Need Nurses*. Mankato, Minn.: Pebble Books, 1999.

On the Web

Kids into Nursing

http://www.unmc.edu/nursing/careers/

For more information about what nurses do and the tools they use

Through the Mail

American Nurses Association

600 Maryland Avenue, S.W.

Suite 100 West

Washington, DC 20024

To write for more information about nursing careers

On the Road

John P. McGovern Museum of Health and Medical Science

1515 Hermann Drive

Houston, TX 77004

713/942-7054

To take a walking tour through the human body at the Amazing Body Pavilion

Index

About the Authors
Cynthia Klingel has worked as a high school English teacher and an elementary school teacher. She is currently the curriculum director for a Minnesota school district. Cynthia Klingel lives with her family in Mankato, Minnesota.

Robert B. Noyed started his career as a newspaper reporter. Since then, he has worked in school communications and public relations at the state and national level. Robert B. Noyed lives with his family in Brooklyn Center, Minnesota.